# *Landscapes*
## *of New Zealand*

*To my wife Sally, who in our 50 years together has always
been quick to spot many great picture opportunities.*

First published in 2003 by New Holland Publishers (NZ) Ltd
Auckland • Sydney • London • Cape Town

218 Lake Road, Northcote, Auckland, New Zealand
14 Aquatic Drive, Frenchs Forest, NSW 2086, Australia
86–88 Edgware Road, London W2 2EA, United Kingdom
80 McKenzie Street, Cape Town 8001, South Africa

www.newhollandpublishers.com

ISBN: 1 86966 025 0

Publishing manager: Renée Lang
Design: Dexter Fry
Editor: Brian O'Flaherty

A catalogue record for this book is available from the National Library of New Zealand

10 9 8 7 6 5 4 3 2

Colour reproduction by Colourscan (Singapore)
Printed by Tien Wah Press (Pte) Ltd

# *Landscapes*
## *of New Zealand*

PHOTOGRAPHY WARREN JACOBS
TEXT JILL WORRALL

KOWHAI

# CONTENTS

ENDPAPERS *Tawny folds of tussock-covered hillside in the Lindis Pass, Central Otago.*
PAGE 1 *A full moon hovers over Lake Hawea and the Southern Alps, Central Otago.*
PAGES 2–3 *First light on Pelorus Sound, Marlborough Sounds.*
LEFT *Kauri trees reach for the light in Trounson Forest, Northland.*
RIGHT *A new fern frond unfolds.*

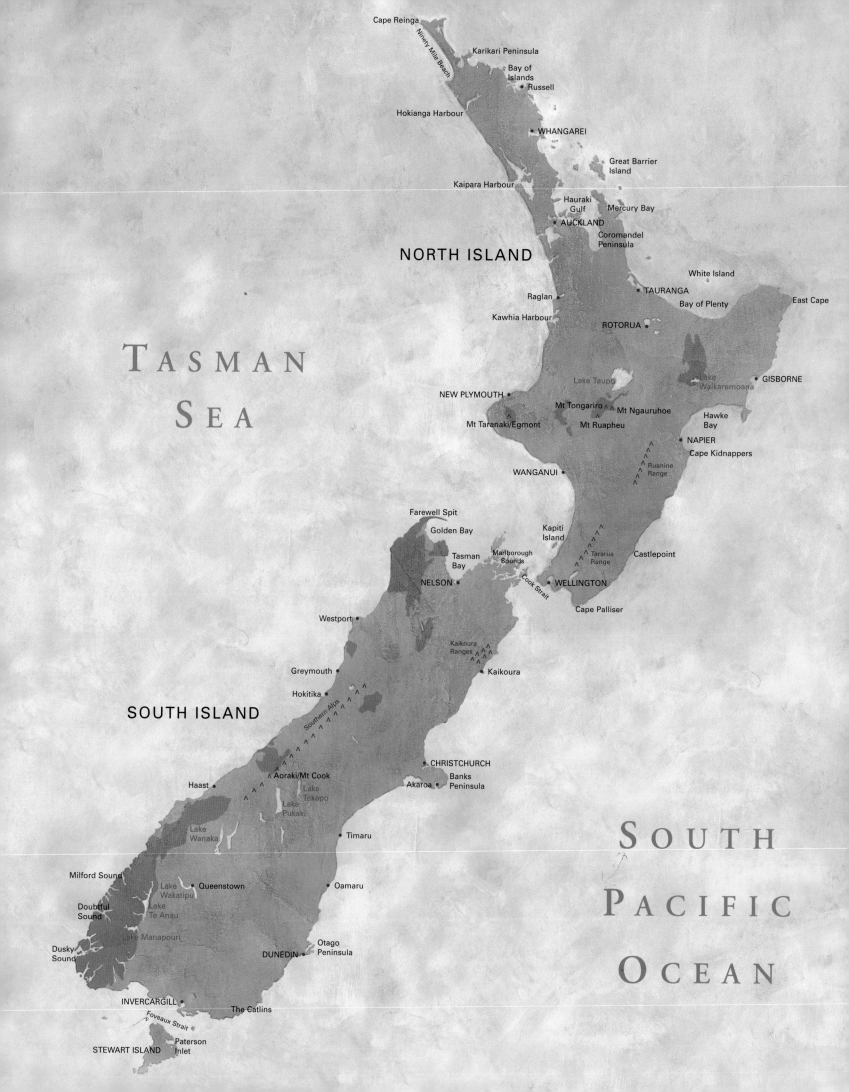

# INTRODUCTION

A fiord at breakfast, a glacier at noon, and a steaming hot pool surrounded by bush-clad mountains as the sun sets. New Zealand may be a small country but within its three main islands is one of the most diverse ranges of landscapes on the planet.

New Zealanders who have grown up in Aotearoa, the Land of the Long White Cloud (as the first settlers, the Maori, named it), take these extraordinary transitions from alpine peaks to forest and tawny expanses of grassland almost for granted. Sometimes it takes the comments of awestruck visitors to reawaken Kiwis' appreciation of their astounding homeland.

But, feeling part of this unique land is something New Zealanders pride themselves on. Even though this is an increasingly urbanised society, most city-dwellers still feel they are closest to the essence of their national identity when they are walking in the forests or along the beach, splashing in a lake or even clinging by their fingertips to the icy sides of a mountain.

The natural forces that have created New Zealand's geological pot-pourri of landforms have also had a major influence on the people who inhabit it.

New Zealanders' mastery of the sea is legendary but the mountains and rivers of the country have also been the training ground for some of the country's most revered citizens. Sir Edmund Hillary, conqueror of Everest, climbed extensively in the South Island's Southern Alps before turning his sights to even higher peaks overseas. World-class athletes, kayakers and rowers have taken to the rivers and hills in their pursuit of excellence. Artists and writers continue to be inspired to explore the landscape and the emotions it engenders.

New Zealand is the largest and most remote group of oceanic islands in the world. What made this outpost of land so diverse?

The causes of this abundance of landscape forms lie beneath the ground. New Zealand's geological history began at least 85 million years ago with the break-up of the New Zealand edge of the supercontinent known as Gondwanaland, and it remains one of the more active (in geological terms) in the world.

Some of the rocks that form its distinctive landscape, however, date back even further (maybe 600 million years) to the country's formation as part of Gondwanaland.

Today, New Zealand lies on a meeting point of two vast tectonic plates, the Indian-Australian and the Pacific, and these constantly moving slabs of the Earth's crust have had greatly different impacts on New Zealand's North and South Islands.

The North Island's smoking and steaming heart, with its volcanoes and thermal areas, is the result of the Indian-Australian Plate riding over the Pacific Plate. As the Pacific Plate sinks, it melts and disintegrates to form superheated magma that erupts to the surface. This violent clash of plates triggers earthquakes, which have also contributed to the shape of the land.

In the South Island the plates are behaving differently – here it is a head-to-head confrontation and as the

plates collide, the land is squeezed. The result is the Southern Alps, the icy, glacier-riven backbone of the island. The mountains are still rising, up to 10 millimetres a year. This is a landscape in the making and this means that the South Island too can be shaken by earthquakes.

Provided with the basic rocky raw materials, other forces have then come into play to fashion the land. Glaciers have gouged into the mountains; erosion by water and wind has sculpted it. Around the nearly 11,000 kilometres of coast, the sea has also been at work – flooding glacial and river valleys, eating away at cliffs and in a natural balancing act, depositing the spoils elsewhere as spits and beaches.

New Zealand's first human inhabitants, the Maori, who probably began to settle the islands around AD 1000 to AD 1200, have their own stories about the origin of Aotearoa.

In Maori mythology, the North Island was hauled from the sea by demigod Maui using a magic fish hook. The island's name in Maori is Te Ika-a-Maui (the fish of Maui) and the origins of many of its landforms are linked to this fishing expedition. Maui's brothers tried to cut up the fish before it was dead and its writhing created the island's rugged hill country and gorges. Lake Taupo, in the centre of the North Island, was the fish's heart, Wellington Harbour its mouth and Northland its tail.

Maui's canoe is the South Island (Te Waka-a-Maui) according to one version of the creation story, with Stewart Island its anchor.

The human inhabitants of New Zealand have not just put their own interpretation on its origins, they've had an effect on the landscape as well.

New Zealand's temperate climate, which has helped form the landscape through unique patterns of wind and precipitation, also provided the perfect environment for the growth of trees – from the temperate rainforests in the south to the subtropical mix of plants in northern areas. Just before human arrival some 78 per cent of the country was forested. One-third of this forest was cleared by pre-European Maori, either intentionally or accidentally, and a further third has been cleared over the last 160 years. Today around 23 per cent

FAR LEFT *Pohutakawa flowering on the Whananaki Coast, Northland.*

LEFT *Mt Tasman at sunset, Aoraki/Mt Cook National Park.*

is still forested – the clearing of the land has been one of the most significant impacts human beings have had on the New Zealand landscape.

Only about 25 per cent of New Zealand lies below 200 metres above sea level, so cities, towns and agriculture have tended to concentrate here. As a result it is these lowland areas where landscapes have been most modified. This has left much of the country's most spectacular landscapes relatively pristine and it is in these places that the largest and most precious tracts of forest survive.

New Zealanders know they live in a beautiful place and millions of overseas visitors now know it too. Unfortunately that has not always stopped humans from damaging what they profess to love. The challenge for the future will be to ensure that New Zealand does not repeat the mistakes of the past and the present, which have led to irreparable damage. The country's landscapes need to be protected so that future generations will also be able to marvel at their extraordinary variety and beauty.

# NORTHLAND
# AUCKLAND
# & COROMANDEL

# 1

# KAURI COUNTRY

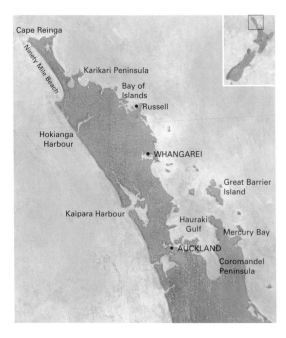

It was the land that first drew both Maori and European settlers to the northernmost part of Aotearoa New Zealand. Land with room and materials for the construction of homes, land ideal for the growing of food, land on which to build a future.

When the first Maori arrived around 1000 years ago after an epic sea journey across the Pacific, they found a pristine landscape, untouched by any human contact, and, growing there, forests of some of the tallest, oldest trees on the planet – the kauri.

To the Europeans who arrived in the 19th century, kauri was more important to the economy of the new nation than gold, and such was demand for timber that they felled the trees almost to the point of extinction. Today, however, the impact of the kauri on the landscape remains in Northland and the Coromandel, whether it is the remnant forests, or the abandoned gumfields (where fossilised kauri resin was dug from the ground) or through its impact on the region's history.

The history of the nation is embedded in the lands of the north. After the first Polynesian settlers landed the next arrivals were Europeans in the early 1800s in search of timber, and whalers looking for fresh water and other supplies. By 1840 New Zealand had become a British colony through the signing of the Treaty of Waitangi in the Far North.

Although it was these historic events on land that were to shape the country in the decades to come, it is impossible to ignore the impact of the sea. Nowhere in Northland, Auckland or Coromandel is far from either the Tasman Sea or the Pacific Ocean. The two bodies of water meet at the country's northern tip just beyond Cape Reinga and sometimes only narrow isthmuses along Northland's heavily indented coastline separate the two. The sea brought the country's inhabitants to its shores and its abundance of fish and other seafood helped sustain the new arrivals and still is an important resource today.

The convoluted coastline, especially on the east coast, is the result of a rise in sea level thousands of years ago, which inundated valleys and lowlands, themselves created mostly by volcanic activity. Northland and the Coromandel Peninsula are the sites of ancient volcanoes and there are around 50 volcanic cones in Auckland, with the youngest, Rangitoto, erupting just 600 years ago.

The proximity of the sea, coupled with a climate that is warm almost year-round, has helped ensure that the northernmost part of New Zealand is the most heavily settled. More than a million people (about a quarter of the country's population) live in the Auckland area and amongst the forests, hills and beaches that lie close by. The natural attractions of Northland and Coromandel attract city dwellers in their thousands at weekends and especially in summer. Despite the influx, these regions manage to retain much of their original tranquillity and allure and remain treasured landscapes.

RIGHT  *The curve of Sandy Bay links Cape Maria van Diemen in the background with Cape Reinga, Northland.*
PREVIOUS PAGES  *The sun rises behind Mt Camel, which stands sentry over the entrance to Houhora Harbour, Northland.*

**ABOVE** *Tiny Maitai Bay lies on the east coast of the remote Karikari Peninsula, home of some of the region's most idyllic beaches.*

**LEFT** *Cape Brett's indented coastline provides many popular anchorages for yachts sailing between Auckland and the Bay of Islands. The craft that can be seen at the top of this photograph are anchored at Whangamumu Harbour. In the foreground is the sweep of Taupiri Bay.*

**BELOW** *Light ripples across a vast expanse of dunes at Te Paki Stream, which trickles across Ninety Mile Beach and into the Tasman Sea.*

**ABOVE**  *Northland's kauri forests once rang with the sound of axes but today the remnants of these forest giants are carefully protected. Kauri can live for more than 2000 years – this tree could well have been growing through every event of human history since the birth of Christ.*

**TOP LEFT**  *The marae (Maori meeting place) at Omanaia sits at the base of the cloud-shrouded Parataiko Range, and close to the Hokianga Harbour.  The churchyard on the small hillock in the centre of the photograph contains rare examples of carved wooden tombstones.*

**BOTTOM LEFT**  *The sheltered natural harbour at Tutukaka is a major centre for game-fishing expeditions.  Just outside the harbour entrance two former New Zealand frigates, the HMNZS* Tui *and* Waikato, *have been sunk, adding to the attractions for divers.*

**BELOW**  *The vineyards on the clay soils at Matakana are some of the most northerly in the country, especially renowned for their red wines.*

**BELOW** *The Waitakere Ranges were once clothed in kauri forest, most of which was plundered almost to oblivion in the 19th century. But the ranges remain a lush green playground for the nearby Auckland metropolis. Reservoirs in the hills also provide the city with vital supplies of fresh water.*

**RIGHT** *Piha Beach, west of the Waitakere Ranges, with its rugged coastline, including the aptly named Lion Rock and black sand beach, is a popular playground for Aucklanders.*

**ABOVE**   *Waiheke Island in the Hauraki Gulf is now within Auckland city's commuter belt, but retains a flavour of its own with a growing number of vineyards and a reputation as a haven for artists.*

**RIGHT**   *Rain clouds gather over Castle Rock on the Coromandel Peninsula. The region was a prime moa-hunting site for the Maori. Later European settlers exploited its abundant kauri, kauri gum and gold.*

**ABOVE** *Square Top island punctuates the coastline near Cape Colville at the northern tip of the Coromandel Peninsula. Captain Cook named the cape after a rear admiral, although he was originally going to call it Cape Egmont.*

**RIGHT** *The pohutukawa flowers in December, so it is often referred to as the nation's Christmas tree. It favours coastal sites and is especially prolific around the Coromandel Peninsula.*

**FAR RIGHT** *The sea has carved out a giant cavern in the rocks at Cathedral Cove (foreground) near Hahei. The headland surrounding the cavern was once a fortified Maori pa.*

# WAIKATO BAY OF PLENTY & VOLCANIC PLATEAU

# 2

# FIRE AND ICE

The heart of the North Island is a testament to the awesome forces that lie beneath the land – a combination of destructive and awe-inspiring power has created many of these regions' distinctive landscapes.

Three volcanoes lie at the centre of the region – Tongariro, Ngauruhoe and Ruapehu – and all three remain active, although each has its own character. Ruapehu (the tallest at 2797 metres) is hundreds of thousands of years old and was responsible for one of New Zealand's worst natural disasters. In 1953 a lahar (a slurry of ice, rocks and mud) broke from the crater lake, thundered down the Whangaehu River and swept away a railway bridge moments before a passenger train arrived; 151 people lost their lives in the crash. Tongariro is also ancient and the least active of the trio, although thermal springs still bubble away on its slopes. Ngauruhoe is the youngest, at about 2500 years old, and with its near-perfect cone displays the classic stratovolcano shape.

To Maori, the mountains have traditionally been the domain of Ruamoko, the god of earthquake and volcanic fire. He believed human beings were trespassers who had to be shaken off the body of his mother Papa (the earth mother). When Maori travelled through the region they averted their eyes from the volcanoes to avoid incurring Ruamoko's wrath.

Today the Waikato is a region of rich pastureland, famed especially for its dairy production, and the region is dominated by its river of the same name. The Waikato is New Zealand's longest river, travelling some 425 kilometres from where it forms the outlet to Lake Taupo to its meeting place with the Tasman Sea. The river's full name is Waikato-taniwha-rau – the flowing water of a hundred taniwha (monsters) – and for Maori it was not just a vital source of food but an important transportation route.

Even this river is influenced by the volcanic activity that has fashioned the landscape. The waters of Lake Taupo are fed by streams flowing from the volcanic heights around it, and the lake itself fills a caldera formed from numerous eruptions, including one, in AD 230, that was the most violent eruption on earth in the last 5000 years. An earlier eruption, 26,500 years ago, was one of the largest ever to occur on the planet.

Although the mountains are the most visible evidence of the activity under the earth's crust, the volcanic area that entices most visitors is Rotorua. Mud pools, thermal springs, geysers and unique landscapes have made it world famous. They provided some of New Zealand's first tourist attractions, and Rotorua still remains one of the country's prime destinations. The city also maintains its role as an important stronghold of Maori culture. The volcanic floorshow is still going strong too – with boiling mud pools occasionally erupting in Rotorua residents' properties.

The sweeping curve of the Bay of Plenty to the north of Rotorua is the fertile antithesis to the often barren, blasted landscapes inland. Fruit grows in lush abundance here, with the warmth and ample sunshine hours proving especially ideal for citrus and kiwifruit – as well as being a magnet for holidaymakers and those looking for a permanent home in the sun.

RIGHT  *Mt Pirongia (a 959-metre extinct basalt volcano) is sacred to the Maori who believe it was the home of patupaiarehe, or fairy people.*
PREVIOUS PAGES  *A full moon hangs above Ngauruhoe, an active volcano in the heart of the North Island.*

**ABOVE** *Steam and sulphurous fumes ooze from the ground at Tikitere (Hell's Gate) in Rotorua, one of the most active thermal areas in the country.*

**RIGHT** *Explosions of superheated mud near Rotorua. The mud is rock broken down by acidic gases produced by volcanic action underground and brought to a boil by thermal activity.*

**ABOVE** *When Mt Tarawera erupted in 1886 the noise could be heard as far away as the South Island. As the mountain tore itself in two the land shuddered with earthquakes and the sky was lit with fireballs. The eruption killed 153 people.*

**LEFT** *Water heated to 75ºC and bubbling with carbon dioxide has created the Champagne Pool at Waiotapu near Rotorua. Silicas, some containing gold and silver, create the striking colours around the pool's margins.*

**ABOVE**  *The might of the Waikato River is forced through a 15-metre wide chasm of rock near Taupo, creating the Huka Falls. The Maori call the falls Hukanui – great body of spray.*

**RIGHT**  *Lake Taupo, New Zealand's largest lake, fills a crater created by volcanic eruptions of awesome proportions.  Today the scene is one of tranquillity and the lake is regarded as one of the best trout fishing spots in the world. Silhouetted at the end of the lake are the volcanoes Ruapehu and Ngauruhoe.*

**ABOVE** *Mt Ruapehu, at 2797 metres the highest of the volcanoes in the Tongariro National Park, is also the area's most active. Ash, steam and even eruptions of rocks are not uncommon. The sulphurous crater near the summit steams constantly.*

**RIGHT** *Livestock graze unconcernedly beneath the bulk of Mt Ruapehu.*

**ABOVE** *The rich volcanic soils around Ohakune are ideal for large-scale cropping. The area used to be known as the Carrot Capital of New Zealand, but now has an increasingly important role catering for visitors to the Volcanic Plateau.*

**RIGHT** *Autumn colours delineate the folds of the Mangawharariki Valley south of Taihape.*

# EAST COAST & HAWKE'S BAY

# 3

# LAND OF FIRST LIGHT

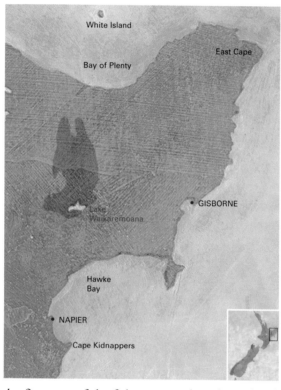

A mysterious rugged, mountainous interior tumbles down to the gently curved beaches and rocky coves of the East Coast and Hawke's Bay.

The remote East Coast, with its spectacular coastal road that flames with the blossom of pohutukawa trees in summer, remains one of the least populated areas in the North Island. The highest mountain on the cape, Mt Hikurangi, is known as the first place in New Zealand to see the light of the new day. The mountain is sacred to Maori, who believe it was the first part of the fish hauled from the sea by Maui – the fish that became the North Island.

This is a Maori heartland too, with the mountains of the Urewera home to the Tuhoe, one of the most traditional of New Zealand tribes, who trace their ancestry back to a meeting of people from the first migration and the fairy people who lived in the hills.

One of New Zealand's most beautiful lakes, Lake Waikaremoana, is the jewel in the crown of the Urewera National Park. The lake was formed around 2000 years ago after a huge landslide blocked waterways and flooded a series of valleys.

This was also the region where the first Europeans set foot in the country. On 9 October 1769, Captain James Cook, botanist Joseph Banks and crew from the *Endeavour* rowed ashore near Gisborne, at the southern end of the East Cape. Their first meeting with the local Maori ended in disaster, with several Maori killed, but subsequent contact between the two races as Cook sailed slowly around the cape, marvelling at its beauty and bounty, were more cordial.

South of Gisborne lies Hawke's Bay, where the early European pioneers cleared much of the native forest to create one of the country's leading pastoral farming areas. Vast sheep stations are found in the hill country and are the origins of much of the traditional wealth of the region. Nearer to the coast the fertile plains have long been used to grow fruit and vegetables. This intensive land use has also shaped the landscape, creating a chequer-board pattern of multi-coloured horticultural produce protected by lines of tall windbreaks. Most recently, the region, which has a Mediterranean-type climate with hot, dry summers, has made a name for itself as one of the country's premier wine-producing areas, especially for the creation of fine chardonnays. The combination of top wines, quality produce and ample sun entice new residents and visitors alike in search of the good life.

RIGHT *Mt Hikurangi on the East Cape is sacred to Maori, and known traditionally as the first place in New Zealand to see the light of a new day.*
PREVIOUS PAGES *Te Mata Peak looms over the Heretaunga Plains and provides sweeping views of Hawke's Bay.*

RIGHT   *Mist hovers above the Waiapu River near Ruatoria, East Cape.*

BELOW   *Rugged hills tumble down to Tokomaru Bay on the East Cape. The bay is named after one of the ancestral canoes Maori believe carried their ancestors to New Zealand from their mythical homeland of Hawaiki.*

BELOW  *A bach (holiday home) with an absolute waterfront location at Waihau Bay on the East Cape.*

RIGHT  *Captain James Cook, during his first exploration of New Zealand in 1769, anchored here in Tolaga Bay. The bay's historic wharf, built in the 1920s, is 660 metres long, and is believed to be the longest in the southern hemisphere.*

FOLLOWING PAGES
LEFT  *A rimu (red pine) of impressive girth flourishing in the Urewera National Park. The native rimu was once common in lowland forest but heavy logging means trees of this magnificence are now all too rare.*

RIGHT  *Luxuriant forest trees, some supported by undulating buttress roots, grow around the shores of Lake Waikaremoana (Sea of Rippling Waters) in the Urewera National Park.*

**RIGHT** *Maori legend recounts how Lake Waikaremoana was formed when a child was deliberately drowned in a spring. But the child turned into a taniwha (monster) and, struggling to escape, formed the great arms of the lake.*

**FAR RIGHT** *The Waipunga Falls cascade through a forest-covered ravine near the Napier-Taupo Highway.*

**BELOW** *The Mohaka River cuts a swathe through the hill country south of the Ureweras, eventually emptying into Hawke Bay.*

**ABOVE** *Market gardens and orchards dominate the plains around the small town of Clive, which lies between Napier and Hastings.*

**LEFT** *Mission Vineyards near Napier was founded by the Marist Brothers (a French Catholic Order) in 1851, making it the country's oldest wine producer still in the same hands.*

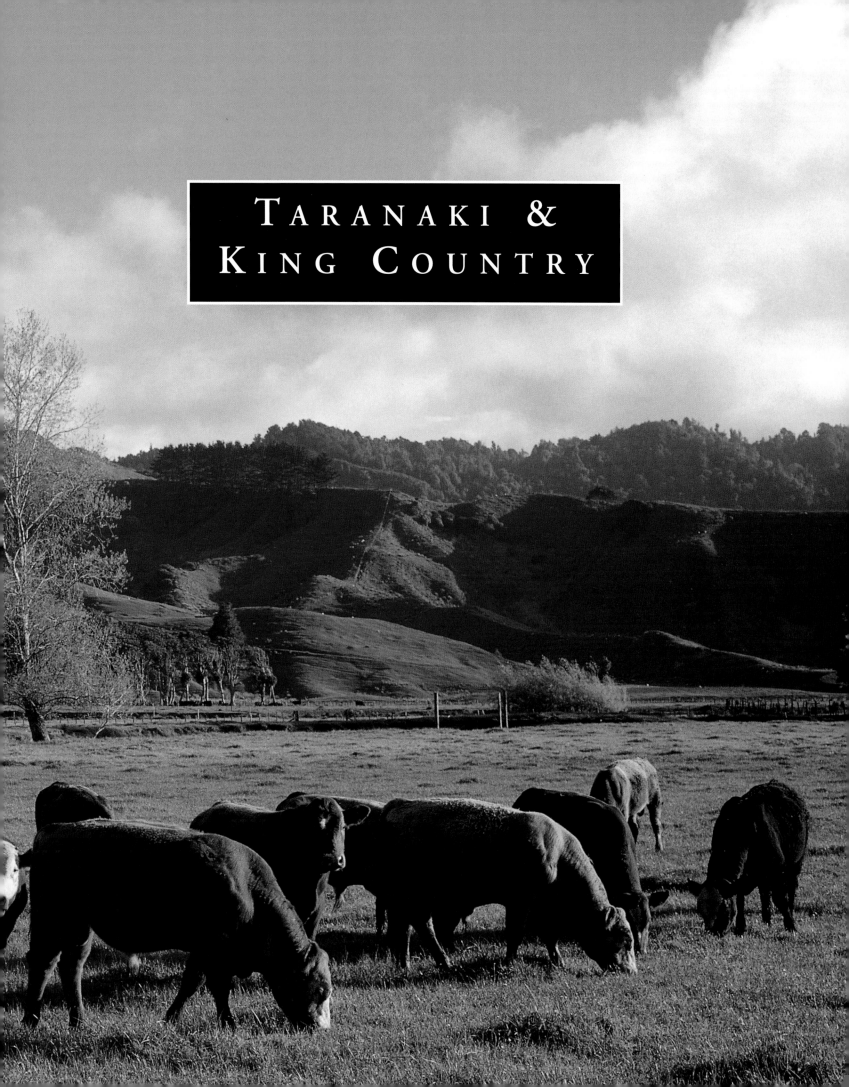

# TARANAKI & KING COUNTRY

# PASTURES GREEN

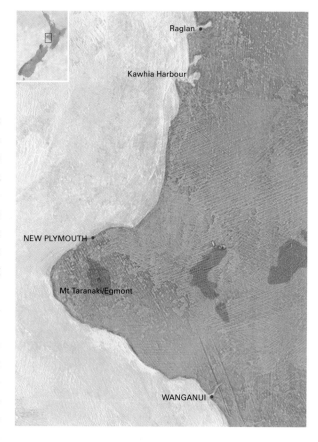

# 4

Raglan

Kawhia Harbour

NEW PLYMOUTH

Mt Taranaki/Egmont

WANGANUI

A tempestuous history of clashes between races links these two regions, which now play vital roles in New Zealand's economy as a leading world producer of agricultural produce. However, while it is a mountain that dominates the Taranaki landscape it is the echoes of history that bind the King Country together.

Mt Taranaki/Egmont provides a spectacular backdrop to the region. The mountain, with its near-perfect cone, is not one volcano but the most dominant cone of a cluster of older volcanoes. Successive eruptions and erosion from these have created the plains that surround it and the rich volcanic soils that have enabled the region to become one of the country's leading producers of dairy products.

Images of cows grazing under the mountain are an enduring image, but this area has not always had such a peaceful demeanour. During the 1860s and 1870s, bitter land wars raged between the Maori inhabitants and the colonial forces.

The Maori legend of how Mt Taranaki/Egmont came to be perched so far to the west of the North Island's volcanic heartland is one of the land's most dramatic. Originally, Taranaki was one of many male volcanoes who lived near Tongariro and his wives, the hills Pihanga and Hauhungatahi. When Tongariro was away, Taranaki seduced Pihanga. However, Taranaki was found out. A confrontation of volcanic proportions ensued and Taranaki fled, carving out the path of the Whanganui River as he did so. He came to rest near the sea, where he became trapped forever.

The origins of the King Country are not so well known or so obvious. This region is named after the Maori King movement that developed during the 1850s and 1860s in response to encroachment by European settlers on to Maori land. Retreating after the land wars of the 1860s, King Tawhiao is said to have dropped a top hat on to a map of the region and declared that the land beneath the hat would remain under his authority. Maori chiefs retained control of this area for decades and Europeans were not allowed to settle there until 1884 – and, for long after, it retained an air of mystery.

Even today the King Country can seem almost a land apart. Its hill country is rugged. Ravines and ridges remain clad in dense forest and the spectacular coastline receives comparatively few visitors. This is pastoral farming territory where urban lifestyles have had little impact.

RIGHT  *Land meets sea in a dramatic line of sandstone cliffs along the Tongaporutu coast in North Taranaki.*
PREVIOUS PAGES  *Agriculture is a thriving industry in Taranaki, thanks to abundant rain and rich volcanic soils.*

**ABOVE**    *The Cape Egmont lighthouse marks the most westerly point in Taranaki. The 66-metre-tall tower was built in 1865 but began life on Mana Island near Cook Strait before being moved to the cape in 1877.*

**LEFT**    *The Dawson Falls are found more than 900 metres up the slopes of Mt Taranaki/Egmont and are easily accessible from Stratford.*

**FAR LEFT**    *The dormant volcano, Mt Taranaki/Egmont, dominates the skyline across the North Taranaki Bight. The black sand beaches of the region are a legacy of volcanic activity.*

**PREVIOUS PAGES**    *Mt Taranaki/Egmont last erupted 350 years ago. Standing 2518 metres high it is known as the most climbed mountain in the country. The mountain is surrounded by a national park established in 1900, the country's second oldest.*

ABOVE *Lake Rotorangi, in southern Taranaki, may look timeless, but was created as a storage lake for hydro-electricity generation.*

RIGHT *The Patea River flows into the Tasman Sea near the southern boundary of Taranaki province. Patea township, at the mouth of the river, was a thriving port during earlier days of European settlement.*

**ABOVE**  *The Whanganui River has been used by both Maori and then European settlers as a route to and from the rugged interior of the central North Island. The river's source is on the volcanic slopes of Mt Tongariro and it flows for 329 kilometres before it meets the sea.*

**RIGHT**  *The Whanganui River flows through the rugged hills near the settlement of Hiruharama (Jerusalem),  which was founded by the Daughters' of Our Lady of Compassion in 1883.*

**FAR RIGHT**  *Lush pasture rather than the original dense native forest now covers much of the hill country inland of Wanganui.*

# MANAWATU & WAIRARAPA

# 5

# HAVEN IN THE HILLS

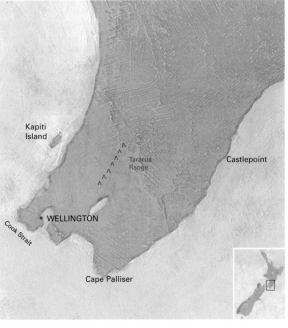

The labels on the map read: Kapiti Island, Tararua Range, Castlepoint, WELLINGTON, Cook Strait, Cape Palliser.

The influence of volcanic activity, a dominant player in most of the North Island's landscapes, loses its sway at the southern end of the island. Here, the long ridges of mountains, such as the Tararua and Rimutaka ranges, are evidence of the mountain-building activity of tectonic plate collision that continues into the South Island.

The link with the south is accentuated along the rocky, indented coastline of the Wairarapa – where, on a clear day the mountains of Te Wai Pounamu (the South Island) stand sentinel across the Pacific Ocean.

The long, central valley of the upper Manawatu River and plains surrounding Masterton are bounded by fault lines. Early European settlers weren't aware of the dramatic origins of this flat land, but made the most of it, clearing the forest for farmland. Unlike the rest of New Zealand, where settlers of British origin dominated the new arrivals in the 19th century, this region has the distinction of being largely developed by thousands of Danish and Norwegian settlers. Their Scandinavian legacy lives on in the names of towns, and especially surnames among the current generation of inhabitants and even in the architecture.

The Wairarapa was one of the earliest parts of New Zealand to be settled by European colonists. Many of these would-be farmers had arrived in Wellington but set off north over the

Rimutaka and Ruahine ranges in search of more promising farming land. They found an area of open plains east of the mountains, separated from the wild, mostly inhospitable coastline by ridge upon ridge of rugged hill country. Both plains and hills proved to be suitable for sheep and the Wairarapa has traditionally been home to millions of them.

Even the rocky, inaccessible stretches of coastline have known the clatter of sheep hooves. It is sometimes easier for farmers to move their flocks along the beach than to negotiate the territory inland. Seafarers in turn often found this coast hazardous; lighthouses such as the one at Castlepoint dot strategic promontories but could not always prevent shipwrecks.

At its southernmost reaches, the region meets the sea near Lake Wairarapa. This was originally an area of significant Maori settlement (the lake's name means Shimmering Waters and was an important food source) but the arrival of Europeans and their demand for land for their sheep brought irreparable change to the original inhabitants' way of life. Many myths prevail, especially concerning the legendary Polynesian navigator Kupe, who is said to have shaken the sea from his feet at Palliser Bay. This bay was named by Captain James Cook, who found the coast awe-inspiring, as do visitors following more than 230 years in his wake.

RIGHT    *Dairying dominates the landscape near Kimbolton inland from Feilding.*

PREVIOUS PAGES    *Pasture gives way to rugged hill country at Mangapakeha in the Wairarapa.*

**LEFT** *Danish settlers in the late 1800s cleared forests for a township called Dannevirke (Danes' Work) and for farmland such as this.*

**ABOVE** *Aerial view of Castlepoint, a former port and now a popular holiday resort as the beach here is one of the few along the rugged Wairarapa coastline. The 23-metre-tall lighthouse was established in 1913.*

**LEFT** *Erosion has worn away the loose silt, sand and shingle from a stretch of hillside near Cape Palliser, creating the Putangirua Pinnacles.*

**FAR LEFT** *New Zealand's State Highway 1, which runs the length of the country, crosses the Rangitikei River, near Mangaweka.*

**LEFT** *Green pasture clothes river lowlands, hills and ridges around Tauweru, east of Masterton, the provincial centre.*

**ABOVE** *Exotic trees and a few sparse natives cast late afternoon shadows over farmland near Masterton.*

**BELOW** *The plains around the Wairarapa town of Masterton are a traditional centre for the production of sheep.*

**BELOW** *Kapiti Island lies just off the coast from Paraparaumu. Once a Maori stronghold, and later a base for whaling stations, the island is now a sanctuary for many of New Zealand's endangered birds.*

**RIGHT** *The narrow plains created by the Ruamahanga River lie under the shadow of the Tararua Range.*

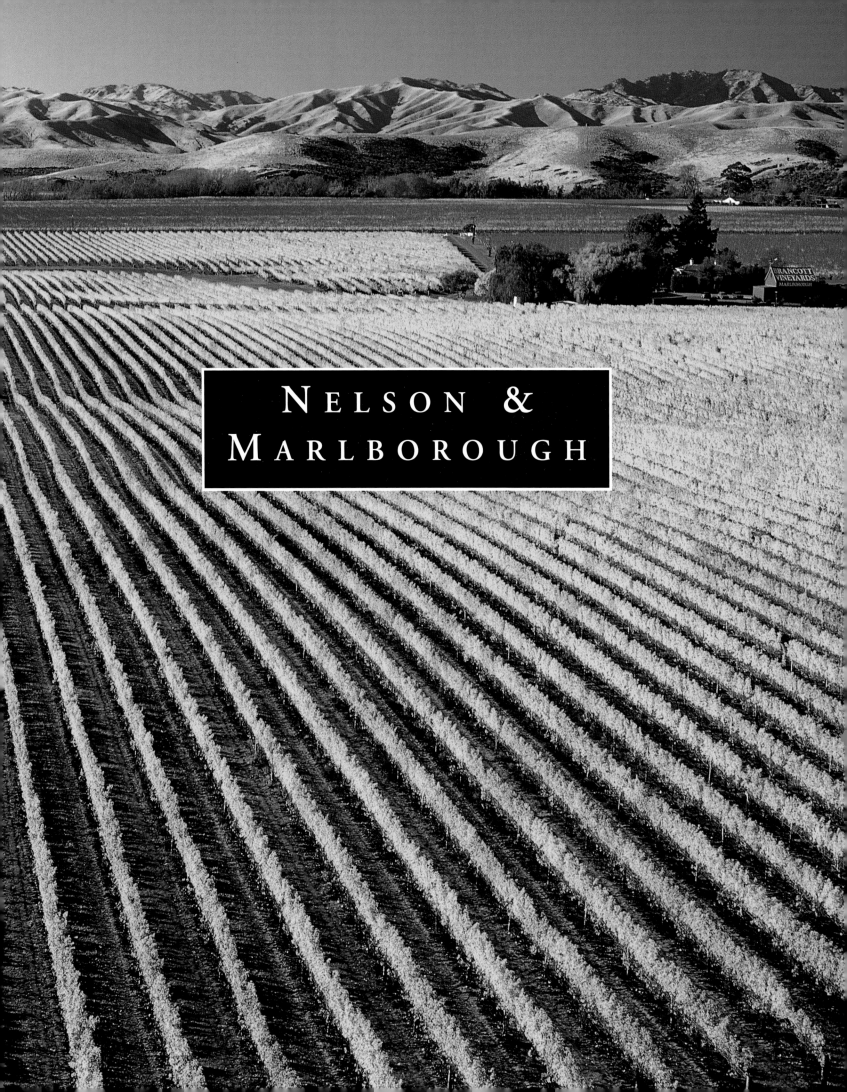

# NELSON & MARLBOROUGH

# 6

# A PLACE IN THE SUN

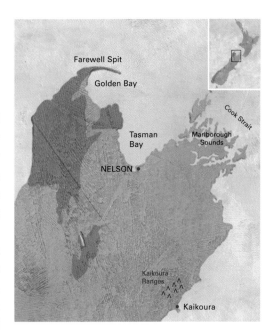

Sunshine, and plenty of it, is a natural resource shared by these two provinces. There is some friendly rivalry between the two districts too, which consistently vie for supremacy at the top of the New Zealand sunshine hours statistics.

Nelson's geological past is a complex mix – some of the oldest, most durable rocks in the country can be found here, but at the farthest north-western corner of the region is Farewell Spit, a hooked finger of sand that is ever-growing and changing.

Maori arrived in Nelson later than in many parts of the North Island. Although their settlements were small in comparison to those further north, the region was the scene of some fierce intertribal warfare – because, just as today, the region's equitable climate, coastal lowland and access to the West Coast and other lands to the south were highly valued.

The attractions of Nelson were not lost on early Europeans either. Nelson was the first organised British settlement in the South Island. The first migrants arrived in 1842 and the region continues to attract new arrivals from around the world as well as New Zealanders lured by the prospect of some of the country's best beaches and high sunshine hours. This eclectic mix has seen the Nelson area garner a growing reputation as a haven for artists and craftspeople as well as cementing its position as a premier area for fruit and hops. It's a region of innovation too with olive trees growing where once more conventional orchards thrived.

To the north-west, Nelson meets the wild West Coast in spectacular fashion – Nelson warmth combines with much wetter weather and the result is luxuriant, almost subtropical forest. To ensure that much of this bountiful and spectacular heritage is preserved for present and future generations, three superb national parks have been created in the region: Kahurangi, Nelson Lakes and Abel Tasman. The last is known around the world for its combination of crystal-clear ocean with golden crescent beaches fringed with forest.

Marlborough is a province famed for its sounds – thousands of kilometres of coastline created when a rise in sea level after the last ice age, combined with land slumping, drowned a complex pattern of river valleys. Maori believe this landscape was the result of a disastrous adventure attempted by a party of gods. They brought a canoe down from heaven but eventually wrecked it. The twisting mountain ridges that rise straight from the sea are all that remains of the carved prow of the gods' canoe.

Inland, Marlborough presents a very different picture. The Wairau Plains around Blenheim, once dominated by sheep, are now striped with row upon row of vines – this is New Zealand's largest wine-growing region and the one that put New Zealand on the world wine map with its sauvignon blancs.

RIGHT *Forest meets golden sand at Totaranui, at the northern end of the Abel Tasman Coastal Track.*
PREVIOUS PAGES *Autumn sets ablaze the extensive vineyards surrounding Blenheim.*

**FAR LEFT** *Te Pukatea Bay in the Abel Tasman National Park can be reached only by foot or by sea, which has helped retain its idyllic combination of forest, golden sand and clear water.*

**TOP LEFT** *Ample rainfall and warm temperatures provide perfect conditions for the growth of the nikau palm, the southern-most palm in the world. These are growing on the Heaphy Track.*

**BOTTOM LEFT** *Water flowing over soft limestone rock of the Takaka hill has, over the centuries, produced fluted, incised pieces of natural art work.*

**TOP**  *The fertile Motueka Valley used to be a prime tobacco-growing area. Still favoured for hop growing, it is a tranquil place, a counterpoint to the summer bustle of coastal Nelson just a few kilometres away.*

**BOTTOM FAR LEFT**  *Motueka's warm and moist climate makes it ideal for the production of one of New Zealand's iconic exports, the kiwifruit. The Arthur Range is on the skyline.*

**BOTTOM RIGHT**  *The narrow strip of land at Riwaka, north of Motueka, has always been farmed intensively. Here, kiwifruit dominate the scene.*

**ABOVE**  *Mt Shewell  looms over the waterways of Pelorus Sound. In the foreground is Fitzroy Bay. The sound was named after the HMS* Pelorus, *which visited in 1838 on a tour of the country's whaling stations. This was the first time the sound had been fully explored.*

**RIGHT**  *Fingers of land stretch into Tasman Bay from a vantage point at French Pass in the Marlborough Sounds. Mussel farming is a thriving industry in these waters – as can be seen in the bay in the foreground.*

**FAR LEFT** *Undulating farmland near Seddon rises rapidly to the slopes of Mt Tapuaenuku, at 2885 metres, the highest peak in the Kaikoura Ranges.*

**LEFT** *The extent of the rugged interior of the Nelson region is obvious from this wintertime aerial view.*

**BELOW** *Although the Nelson region is almost synonymous with beaches, its inland attractions include Lake Rotoiti (Maori for Little Lake), formed as the glaciers in the region retreated.*

**RIGHT** *Mountains meet the ocean in dramatic fashion at Kaikoura on the South Island's east coast. The settlement of Kaikoura lies on a tiny peninsula which, according to Maori legend, was the seat on which Maui sat when he heaved the North Island up from the sea.*

**BELOW** *Dairy cattle thrive on the narrow strip of coastal land at Kaikoura.*

# CANTERBURY

# 7

# FROM PLAIN TO PEAK

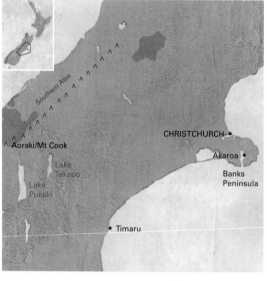

A region of diverse landscapes, Canterbury encompasses the country's highest peaks, its most extensive coastal plains and a long, often lonely, stretch of coastline. Cantabrians, regarded as some of the most parochial residents in the country, know that with a little planning they can be skiing on a glacier at first light and be dabbling their toes in the Pacific by late afternoon.

Awesome subterranean upheavals have created the Southern Alps that form the backbone of the region. New Zealand's highest mountain, Aoraki/Mt Cook (3754 metres), and 16 other peaks that reach more than 3000 metres. They are the creation of the clash of two tectonic plates, which has heaved up huge slabs of greywacke rock. This process is ongoing, with the Southern Alps rising at a rate of up to 10 millimetres a year. Erosion in the form of glaciers and the action of wind and rain has left its mark too. Retreating rivers of ice gouged out troughs now filled by elongated lakes such as Tekapo and Pukaki and over the millennia gravels washed out of the mountains have created the Canterbury Plains.

As the gravels spread they settled and linked forever the mainland and the volcanic outpost of Banks Peninsula. Captain Cook, who sailed past in 1770, mistook the peninsula for an island; it is in fact the eroded remnants of two extinct volcanoes. Their final eruptions were so violent the sides of their craters blew out and the sea flooded in, creating two spectacular natural harbours, Lyttelton and Akaroa.

The first European setters sailed into Lyttelton in 1850 and climbed the steep Bridle Path over the lip of the ancient crater, and down on to the plains. There they established what is today the South Island's largest city, Christchurch. Once on the plains they were following in the footsteps of the island's first human inhabitants, Maori moa hunters, who had long before set fire to much of the lowland forest in order to flush out the massive flightless birds.

Maori did venture into the mountains, discovering the first passes through to the West Coast. They named the highest peak Aoraki. According to one Maori legend the mountain is one of the sons of Raki (the sky) and Papa (the earth). Aoraki and his brothers came down to earth in their canoe, which capsized. The brothers climbed on to the high side of their craft and were transformed into stone and earth – Aoraki was the tallest of the brothers.

Today the mountains are largely the domain of recreationalists and extensive flocks of sheep, and this is the home of high-country sheep stations. On the plains, once one of the most important cereal growing areas in the country (with farmers often combining cropping with sheep), there have been some dramatic changes. Extensive irrigation networks, using water from the wide braided rivers flowing from the Alps, have seen the arrival of thousands of dairy cattle. There are vineyards too, especially in North Canterbury and, appropriately, around Akaroa on Banks Peninsula. Appropriately, because this was the scene of France's attempt to colonise the country. The British had beaten them to it, but the French settlers stayed on.

RIGHT *Autumn fires up the hills and river flats of the Greta Valley in North Canterbury.*
PREVIOUS PAGES *Snow blankets the pastures of Glenmore Station on the shores of Lake Tekapo.*

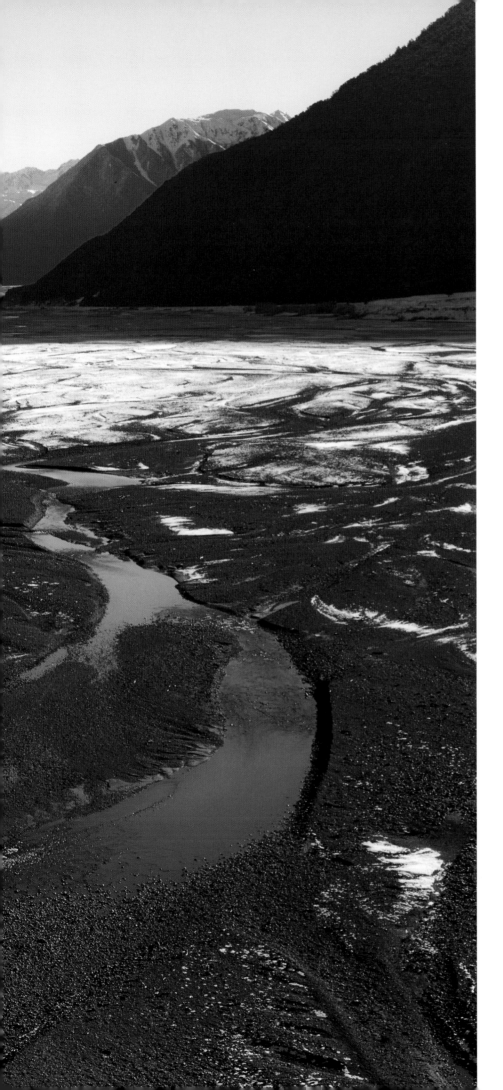

LEFT   *The Waimakariri (Cold River) rises in the Southern Alps near Arthur's Pass (towards the top right of the photograph) and flows 161 kilometres through a series of braided channels to the Pacific Ocean, just north of Christchurch.*

BELOW   *An alpine stream tumbles through the Crow Valley in Arthur's Pass National Park.*

**RIGHT** *Sheep have adapted well to life in the South Island high country. This flock is wintering out on lower pastures at Castle Hill, Canterbury. The Craigieburn Range is in the background.*

**BELOW** *Lake Pearson lies between Porters Pass and Arthur's Pass in the Southern Alps.*

**ABOVE**  *Lyttelton Harbour on Banks Peninsula is a drowned volcanic crater. Captain James Cook named the peninsula after botanist Sir Joseph Banks who sailed with him around New Zealand in 1770.*

**FAR LEFT**  *Governors Bay at the head of Lyttelton Harbour. The first wave of European pioneers who established Christchurch sailed into this harbour in 1850.*

**LEFT**  *Akaroa Harbour on Banks Peninsula. French settlers arrived here in 1840, but sovereignty had already been claimed by the British. However the French stayed and their influence remains today.*

**ABOVE** *New Zealand's highest peak, Aoraki/Mt Cook (3754 metres) looms over the Tasman Glacier (foreground). Mt Tasman, the country's second highest mountain (3497 metres), is in the centre.*

**RIGHT** *Lake Pukaki fills a valley gouged out long ago by the Tasman Glacier. Now it forms a backdrop for Aoraki/Mt Cook, centre, and its attendant peaks, the largest concentration of 3050-metre-plus mountains in the country.*

**FAR LEFT** *Moonrise over Lake Pukaki in the Mackenzie Basin. The lake level has been raised as part of an extensive hydro-electricity scheme in the basin.*

**ABOVE** *The still waters of Lake Tekapo reflect the snow-dusted tops of the Two Thumb Range, also known locally as the Richmond Range.*

**LEFT** *Tranquillity steals in with the winter at Lake Alexandrina, a favoured fishing spot, which lies alongside the much larger Lake Tekapo.*

# WEST COAST

# 8

# SPLENDID ISOLATION

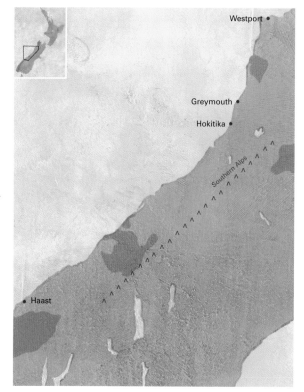

Westport •

Greymouth •

Hokitika •

Southern Alps

• Haast

Ever since early Maori first visited the West Coast in search of highly prized greenstone (jade), travel to the South Island's narrow western coastal strip has always presented a challenge.

There are few ways through the mountains and even today passes can often be closed due to snow or heavy rain. Largely isolated from the rest of the country in this way, Coasters (as its residents are affectionately known) have developed a special character, largely by a lifestyle that until recently has almost entirely depended on the hard physical work of utilising the region's natural resources of coal, gold and timber.

There is little flat land wedged between an often tumultuous Tasman Sea and the Southern Alps – at its widest point it is just 50 kilometres from mountain peak to ocean. Much of the land is still clad in podocarp forest (although milling has had a significant impact in some areas). This lush rainforest owes its existence to the mountains. They halt the progress of east-moving clouds, which then drop their rain in vast quantities – about five metres a year.

Gold was discovered on the Coast in 1864, sparking one of the biggest gold rushes in the Pacific, enticing more than 16,000 miners from around the world. Today, gold is still mined on a much smaller scale but the populations in many of the former gold rush towns have dwindled. Coal was also found in quantities in the region, and it too brought short-term economic prosperity for many small settlements. Only a few mines remain but the lasting legacy of both coal and gold can still be seen in lichen-covered mounds of tailings and long-abandoned mining equipment rusting slowly away in forest clearings. There is a strong sense of the past here, more tangible on the Coast perhaps than in many other parts of the country.

Today, the Coast looks increasingly towards tourism for its economic well-being. Spectacular coastal scenery, including the limestone wonders at Punakaiki, and the Franz Josef and Fox Glaciers, are major drawcards. Nowhere else in the world at this latitude do glaciers flow down so close to the sea.

In the south of the region, retreating glaciers have created deep troughs now filled by a series of lakes. Tall podocarp trees fringe their shores and beyond rise the western ramparts of the Southern Alps, creating quintessential images of Aotearoa New Zealand.

RIGHT   *The Tasman Sea makes landfall at Meybille Bay north of Punakaiki.*
PREVIOUS PAGES   *Limestone cliffs and luxuriant rainforest combine beside the Pororari River in the Paparoa National Park.*

**FAR LEFT** *Wave action and ample rainfall over millions of years have gnawed away at the foundations of the coast, creating the distinctive limestone landscape at Punakaiki, creating blowholes and the unique Pancake Rocks.*

**LEFT** *Northern rata, one of New Zealand's largest flowering trees, flourish in the wet, temperate conditions of the Paparoa National Park. These trees can reach up to 30 metres tall. According to Maori myth the flowers are the blood of spirit ancestor Tawhaki.*

**ABOVE** *Many of New Zealand's 200 or more species of fern flourish on the West Coast. The silver fern has been adopted as one of the country's national emblems.*

**RIGHT** *Lake Kaniere, which is surrounded by low-land podocarp forest, is just inland from the historic former goldmining town of Hokitika.*

**BELOW** *A stand of swamp kahikatea or white pine, fringing Lake Wahapo, just north of Franz Josef Glacier.*

**BOTTOM RIGHT** *Lake Mapourika is one of many Westland lakes created after a major glacial retreat about 14,000 years ago. Huge slabs of ice were left behind, insulated by a thick layer of moraine. Once the ice finally melted the gravels collapsed inwards, creating the lakes.*

**FOLLOWING PAGES** *Quintessential New Zealand – this is possibly the most photographed scene in the entire country. The peaks of Aoraki/Mt Cook (right) and Mt Tasman (left) are reflected in the serene waters of Lake Matheson.*

**ABOVE**  *Explorer and geologist Julius von Haast was one of the first Europeans to set foot on the Fox Glacier. It is the largest glacier in New Zealand, a river of ice stretching about 13 kilometres from its source in the Southern Alps down to about 300 metres above sea level.*

**LEFT**  *Mt Tasman and the ice and snow fields at the head of the Fox Glacier, which are fed by water-laden westerly winds. The glacier has been on the move since 1985 and in the 10 years up to about 2000 had advanced about 1 kilometre.*

**RIGHT** *Strong prevailing westerly winds and often heavy seas keep West Coast beaches, like this one at Bruce Bay, well stocked with driftwood and other ocean-borne debris.*

**BELOW RIGHT** *Rock pinnacles adrift off the coastline at Knights Point – the point was named after the dog of a surveyor who worked on this spectacular stretch of highway.*

**FAR RIGHT** *The Haast Past, which links South Westland with Central Otago over the Southern Alps, was used by Maori long before it was rediscovered by Charles Cameron in 1863. The road through the pass, which opened in 1965, took 30 years to build.*

OTAGO

# 9

# HEART OF GOLD

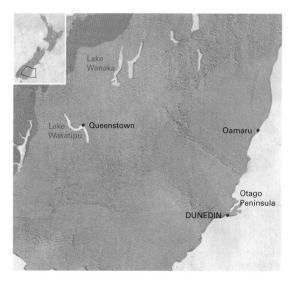

Gold in the hills and in the rivers lured thousands of early prospectors into the heart of Central Otago. They've long gone now but today it's the gold of the tussock and the burning colours of autumn that live on in the landscape.

Otago can claim its own stretches of sublime coastline but some of its most distinctive landscapes lie inland. Central Otago is a region of dramatic schist outcrops, rolling expanses of tussock, alpine lakes and on its westernmost boundary, the Southern Alps.

The metamorphic rock, formed under intense heat and pressure below the ground long ago, forms the foundation of the landscape, which in turn has been shaped by some of the most extreme climatic conditions in New Zealand. Summers can be searingly hot and dry, the warmth drawing out the scent of wild thyme from the hills, and winters can be the coldest in the country, –20°C has been recorded in Ophir, near Alexandra.

Linking the lakes and mountains of Central Otago and the more fertile, lusher Otago coastal areas is the Clutha River, one of New Zealand's largest rivers and the one that carries the greatest volume of water. Today it is dammed in several places for hydro-electric power. The largest of these dams at Clyde has created one of New Zealand's newest lakes, Lake Dunstan.

Maori moa hunters roamed the once forested hills of Otago and their settlements along the coast were, in pre-European times, some of the most densely populated in the country. But this had all changed by the time the first Europeans arrived – the moas had been hunted to extinction (and in the process much of the forest had been destroyed) and a cooling of the climate had made growing many traditional Polynesian crops impossible.

The first sizeable population of Europeans arrived from Scotland in 1848. Their impact on the region remains strong: descendants of these original settlers cherish their heritage, even the presence of stone walls harks back to the crofts of the Scottish highlands.

Gold was discovered in 1861 and the region's population expanded from a mere 12,000 souls to more than 50,000, most of them miners. The coastal city of Dunedin mushroomed in proportion to the growing quantities of gold being won from the ground and for many decades it economically outshone the other main centres. But by the early 1900s the boom was over and now it is tourists who provide the new gold, especially in the Queenstown region, which is world renowned for its adventure tourism set in a spectacular alpine landscape.

Despite the numbers of visitors, the region remains characterised by a sense of space – enticing to some, forbidding to others. It's a place of vast skies and dramatic seasonal changes that gives way near the coast to a gentler, softer landscape.

RIGHT  *The tussock-clad folds of the hills that flank the Lindis Pass, linking Central Otago and the Mackenzie Basin.*
PREVIOUS PAGES  *A craggy outcrop surrounded by a sea of tussock near the Old Dunstan Road in Central Otago.*

**ABOVE** *The construction of the Clyde Dam on the Clutha River between 1977 and 1989 led to the creation of Lake Dunstan.*

**LEFT** *Early morning light accentuates the barrenness of the landscape of Central Otago along the Old Dunstan Road. The road, now a four-wheel-drive track, was first used in 1862 by thousands of gold miners hoping to strike it rich in the goldfields of The Dunstan (now known as Clyde).*

BELOW   *Glendhu Bay in a sheltered corner of Lake Wanaka. The lake is the source of one of New Zealand's longest rivers, the Clutha.*

RIGHT   *Although the Wanaka area, with its reputation for adventure tourism and superb scenery, is now a major tourist destination, farming is still an important part of the economy.*

**FAR LEFT**  *The Shotover River snakes through the Skippers Canyon, near Queenstown. The journey up the 28-kilometre road is regarded as one of the country's great white-knuckle drives and follows the route gold miners used in the 1860s.*

**ABOVE**  *Vineyards are a relatively new feature of the Central Otago landscape. This one is on the sunny slopes above Lake Hayes.*

**LEFT**  *Central Otago icons – glistening schist rock and autumn leaves.*

PREVIOUS PAGES

LEFT  *Meiklejohns Bay on Lake Wakatipu, with Mt Earnslaw in the background.*

RIGHT  *Winter in Central Otago means curling, a game brought to New Zealand from Scotland in 1873 and taken up with a passion by the early gold miners. Smooth cottage-loaf-shaped rounds of granite are slid along the ice in a game that has similarities to outdoor bowls.*

ABOVE  *Roxburgh's river flats and gentle hill country, irrigated with water from the Clutha River, produce both livestock and fruit. The area is especially famed for its apricots.*

RIGHT  *The Clutha River carries the most water of any river in New Zealand and has a history closely linked with that of the gold miners who were some of the earliest European settlers in the region.*

LEFT *An aerial view of the rugged, sparsely populated hills of East Otago.*

BOTTOM LEFT *Schist, the ubiquitous rock of Central Otago, was put to many uses by early settlers. As it split into layers easily it could even be used to create stone sheepyards. In a region where trees are scarce and the climate harsh, the schist was an ideal alternative.*

BELOW *Lake Mahinerangi is a manmade lake created inland of Dunedin to provide the city with its own hydro-electric power and has generated power since 1926.*

# FIORDLAND & SOUTHLAND

# 10

# GRAND FINALE

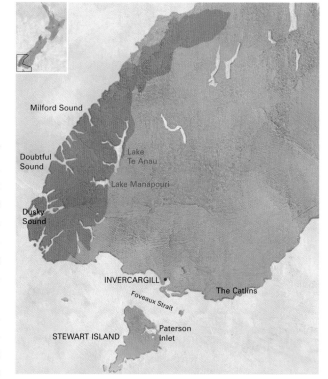

The extreme south of New Zealand, almost the final fling of the chain of islands that stretch through the Pacific, offers some of the mostly highly modified rural landscapes in the country juxtaposed with one of the planet's most magnificent wilderness areas.

Fiordland is the least populated region in the country and with good reason. Metamorphic rock heaved from the earth's crust was later overlaid with massive ice sheets and glaciers that gouged their way to the sea. When these rivers of ice retreated they left behind steep-sided valleys which were flooded by the ocean. There are few places where humans can settle, and the climate still presents its own challenges – yearly rainfall of over 6.5 metres is not uncommon.

Almost entirely protected within New Zealand's largest national park, Fiordland is awe-inspiring, remote and a place that retains an aura of mystery. With so much mountainous terrain still untrodden by humans, it is no surprise that legends of lost Maori tribes, strange beasts, and sightings of the extinct moa abound here.

Maori hunters explored this region but have left few reminders of their presence. They believed the god Tu used his adze to create a carved landscape that would last forever.

Ironically, despite its isolation, Fiordland has an important part to play in the history of New Zealand's European settlement. Captain James Cook and his crew aboard the *Resolution* spent more than six weeks in Dusky Sound, and it is still possible to see the stumps of trees cut down to provide wood for repairs to the ship. Anchor Island, at the entrance to the sound, was the site of the first known European building in the country – a sealers hut built in 1792.

The glaciers that created the fiords also left behind deep troughs now filled by lakes, including the South Island's largest lake, Te Anau, and its stunningly beautiful neighbour, Manapouri.

The rolling pastures of Southland present a much less forbidding scene. Although spared the deluges of rain that drop on Fiordland, this region is still well watered, making it ideal for large-scale dairying. The province meets the Pacific Ocean along the Catlins coast where precious remnants of eastern lowland forest can be explored. There are beaches in the south too. Hardy Southlanders (many of whom share Scottish ancestry with Otago residents) have built holiday homes where the view can stretch far into the Southern Ocean – next landfall Antarctica.

RIGHT *Rain clouds lifting to reveal Mitre Peak on Milford Sound.*
PREVIOUS PAGES *MV* Tawera*, which was built in 1899, tied up at a jetty on Lake Te Anau.*

**TOP LEFT** *Winter feed sustains sheep grazing in the Eglinton Valley, the gateway for motorists heading to Milford Sound from Te Anau.*

**ABOVE** *The Eglinton River flows into Lake Te Anau, helping to fill New Zealand's second largest lake after Lake Taupo in the North Island.*

**LEFT** *Almost the entire stretch of Lake Te Anau's 500 kilometres of shoreline is uninhabited. And in 1948 beyond the far shores, high in the Murchison Mountains, the flightless bird the takahe, long thought to be extinct, was rediscovered.*

**LEFT** *Charles Sound is a remote and rarely visited fiord north of Doubtful Sound. Beyond the head of the Emelius Arm of the fiord towers 1879-metre Mount Irene.*

**BELOW** *Serene Lake Manapouri belies a turbulent recent past when thousands of New Zealanders during the 1960s and early 70s battled a government determined to raise lake levels as part of an ambitious hydro-electric power scheme. The lake was never raised.*

**ABOVE** *More than six metres of rain falls annually in Fiordland, creating thousands of waterfalls, from roaring monsters to ephemeral cascades.*

**RIGHT** *Luxuriant rainforest forms an almost impenetrable barrier to movement around the shores of Doubtful Sound. The sound was named in 1770 by Captain James Cook, who sailed past the entrance because he was doubtful that, should he venture in, there would be sufficient wind to get out again.*

**ABOVE**  *The Takitimu Mountains form some of the eastern ramparts of Fiordland, separating the wild remote south-west from the more gentle, agricultural land of Southland.*

**LEFT**  *There's no road into Long Point, a lonely rocky headland on Fiordland's southern coast. Set off due south by sea from here and the next landfall is likely to be Antarctica.*

**FAR LEFT**  *Seagulls hover behind a tractor working the narrow plain at Five Rivers, wedged between the Eyre and Garvie mountains, north of Lumsden.*

**ABOVE** *Porpoise Bay in the Catlins takes its name from the rare Hector's dolphins that often play in the waves here. Penguins, seals and sea lions are also regular visitors.*

**LEFT** *It might be called Cosy Nook but this tiny settlement clinging to the rocks west of Invercargill is face to face with the might of the Southern Ocean.*

**FOLLOWING PAGE** *Black Point lies south-east of Invercargill near one of the country's most scenic touring routes through the Catlins. Just a stone's throw from this remote promontory is Slope Point, the most southerly point in the South Island.*